Written by Craig Robert Carey
Illustrated by Isidre Mones

Rescue Action

SCHOLASTIC INC.

New York Toronto London Auckland Sydney
Mexico City New Delhi Hong Kong Buenos Aires

HASBRO and its logo and TONKA are trademarks of Hasbro and are used with permission.
© 2006 Hasbro. All Rights Reserved.

Published by Scholastic Inc.
SCHOLASTIC and associated logos are trademarks and/or registered trademarks of Scholastic Inc.

ISBN 0-439-83011-7

12 11 10 9 8 7 6 5 4 3 2 1   6 7 8 9 10/0

Printed in the U.S.A.
First printing, August 2006

Designed by Phil Falco

When firefighters need to reach a high window or rooftop, **ladder trucks** get to work. The powerful ladders on these vehicles can lift firefighters more than ten stories high!

The platform at the top of most ladder trucks allows firefighters to get in close to the action. Hose nozzles on the platform spray gallons of water on the fire below!

The **coast guard boat** is used for
superfast rescues and police actions at sea.

The fireboat does double duty, helping the fire trucks fight blazes on dry land. If a building near a river or lake is on fire, the fireboat can pump right from the water and use its powerful hoses to put out the flames!

When a mountain rescue is needed, the **rescue helicopter** is on the job! It hovers by the scene of the accident and uses its hoists to lift people to safety.

The rescue action can also happen inside the copter. Some rescue helicopters are like flying hospitals with room for as many as 16 patients!

Some forest fires occur so far away from roads that fire trucks can't reach them. That's when it's time to fight fire from the sky with the **firefighting aircraft**!

Firefighting planes and helicopters carry both water and special chemicals to help put out fires. The planes can carry 15,000 gallons at a time — that's as much as a swimming pool holds!

The **interceptor** is the fastest vehicle on the police squad. It can race down almost any car on the road!

The interceptor is equipped with a speed-checking radar and two-way radios. That way the police can call ahead to one another to trap a speeding driver!

Hazmat trucks carry special tools to clean up dangerous spills. *Hazmat* is short for *hazardous materials*. That means *stay back!*

When there's a fire at the airport, call out the **ARFF**! ARFF stands for Aircraft Rescue and Fire Fighting.

Many ARFF trucks have special hose nozzles with sharp metal tips attached. These can cut through the outside of the plane to put out fires in enclosed spaces.

Whenever there's trouble, these vehicles race into action — RESCUE ACTION!